Samuel French Acting Edition

Klook and Vinette

by Ché Walker

Music by Omar Lyefook & Anoushka Lucas

Copyright © 2019 by Ché Walker, Omar Lyefook, Anoushka Lucas
All Rights Reserved

KLOOK AND VINETTE is fully protected under the copyright laws of the United States of America, the British Commonwealth, including Canada, and all other countries of the Copyright Union. All rights, including professional and amateur stage productions, recitation, lecturing, public reading, motion picture, radio broadcasting, television and the rights of translation into foreign languages are strictly reserved.

ISBN 978-0-573-70756-8

www.SamuelFrench.com
www.SamuelFrench.co.uk

FOR PRODUCTION ENQUIRIES

UNITED STATES AND CANADA
Info@SamuelFrench.com
1-866-598-8449

UNITED KINGDOM AND EUROPE
Plays@SamuelFrench.co.uk
020-7255-4302

Each title is subject to availability from Samuel French, depending upon country of performance. Please be aware that *KLOOK AND VINETTE* may not be licensed by Samuel French in your territory. Professional and amateur producers should contact the nearest Samuel French office or licensing partner to verify availability.

CAUTION: Professional and amateur producers are hereby warned that *KLOOK AND VINETTE* is subject to a licensing fee. Publication of this play(s) does not imply availability for performance. Both amateurs and professionals considering a production are strongly advised to apply to Samuel French before starting rehearsals, advertising, or booking a theater. A licensing fee must be paid whether the title(s) is presented for charity or gain and whether or not admission is charged. Professional/Stock licensing fees are quoted upon application to Samuel French.

No one shall make any changes in this title(s) for the purpose of production. No part of this book may be reproduced, stored in a retrieval system, or transmitted in any form, by any means, now known or yet to be invented, including mechanical, electronic, photocopying, recording, videotaping, or otherwise, without the prior written permission of the publisher. No one shall upload this title(s), or part of this title(s), to any social media websites.

For all enquiries regarding motion picture, television, and other media rights, please contact Samuel French.

MUSIC USE NOTE

Licensees are solely responsible for obtaining formal written permission from copyright owners to use copyrighted music in the performance of this play and are strongly cautioned to do so. If no such permission is obtained by the licensee, then the licensee must use only original music that the licensee owns and controls. Licensees are solely responsible and liable for all music clearances and shall indemnify the copyright owners of the play(s) and their licensing agent, Samuel French, against any costs, expenses, losses and liabilities arising from the use of music by licensees. Please contact the appropriate music licensing authority in your territory for the rights to any incidental music.

IMPORTANT BILLING AND CREDIT REQUIREMENTS

If you have obtained performance rights to this title, please refer to your licensing agreement for important billing and credit requirements.

KLOOK AND VINETTE was first produced by Steven Rinkoff for Vaultage Productions at Park Theatre in London, England on June 11, 2014. The performance was directed by Ché Walker, with music direction by Anoushka Lucas, lighting design by Arnim Friess, choreography by Patience James. The cast was as follows:

KLOOK	Ako Mitchell
VINETTE	Sheila Atim
THE MUSICIAN	Rio Kai

KLOOK AND VINETTE was produced by Lisa Adler and Jeff Adler at Horizon Theatre Company in Atlanta, Georgia on January 19, 2018. The performance was directed by Ché Walker, with music direction by Christian Magby, set design by Isabel and Moriah Curley-Clay, lighting design by Mary Parker, costume design by Dr. L Nyrobi Moss, projection design by Bobby Johnston, and sound design by Rob Brooksher. The props master was Kathryn Muse and the movement collaborator was Nicole Johnson. The production stage manager was Julianna Lee, and the rehearsal assistant stage manager was Kayla Zinke. The cast was as follows:

KLOOK	Amari Cheatom
VINETTE	Brittany Inge
THE MUSICIAN	Christian Magby / Maurice Figgins

CHARACTERS
KLOOK
VINETTE

SETTING

Somewhere in America, most likely Stockton, California

TIME

Now

*For Reg E. Cathey, in loving memory,
and for Linda Powell*

[MUSIC NO. 01 "MEMORIES"]

KLOOK.
>MEMORIES CASCADING,
>FAKING MASQUERADING,
>WHAT IS REAL, WHAT IS TRUE?
>NEON SIGN FLIPS RED TO BLUE
>
>LONELINESS TIES ME IN CHAINS,
>SHIVER NAKED IN THE RAIN
>I'VE LIVED MY LIFE IN CRUELTY,
>LIKE I'M IN A GANGSTER MOVIE, YEAH
>
>MEMORIES,
>MAKE A MOCKERY
>MEMORIES
>KEEP ON FUCKIN' ME
>
>HOUNDED BY THE MEMORIES,
>
>WONDER IF I'M CURSED
>SEARCHING FOR THE WORDS,
>WHILE I FUMBLE FOR REVERSE
>
>SOMETHING HEREDIT'RY
>GHOST IN THE FAMILY
>WHY'D THIS END UP SO UNHAPPILY
>
>AND THE WHITE LINES
>GOT ME CHASING THEM WHITE LINES
>AND CAT'S EYES
>BLINDED BY THE WHITE LINES

Bottle of rum in one hand.

Gun in the other.

Benzedrine and adrenaline make a monster in my veins.

Rickety old fan swirling in the motel room.

Red and blue lights.

Woo woo of sirens.
Whump whump of helicopter blades.
I am unlikely to live another day.

(Music out.)

Man, if anybody had told me I'd be sticking a gun through a Venetian blind and firing into a flotilla of police cars, I'd a said you crazy now why I'd go and do that? Not for the first time, I wonder juss what in the fuck went wrong? Because whoever decides this shit... Whoever actually is in charge, politics, God, universal laws, biological determinism, whatever the fuck... It has become plain to see that my cards have been marked for the longest time... Don't matter if I duck and twist this way and that and cover up with both hands on the ropes... This world been a kaleidoscope of spiritual uppercuts, for the most part...

Could never make my life into what I wanted it to be, y'know? Thass 'cause, truth be told, I never knew what it was I wanted to do with it... No patience, thass me.

Bounced around from town to town drifting, grifting, heavy lifting, and could never settle on a job or a home or a woman.
Life of peripatetic propulsion and a nagging loneliness.
Pretty much resigned to it.
Getting old.
Who gives a shit? Solitude is not so bad, means you can get some things straight in your mind, y'know?
Not so bad.

MEMORIES KEEP ON FUCKING ME...

I'm in one a them kinda joints white dudes with dreadlocks and rings through their noses.

I liked to go in there 'cause I'm wary of all the chemicals they spray in the fruit and these white dreadlock dudes look like they were on top a that. Ecological brothers, y'know?

Sitting down at the counter, revisiting *Notes From The Underground* and munching on a modestly vivacious quinoa sweet pepper and broccoli medley, thinking 'bout work later, juss standard procedure...

Door swing open...

And then there was she.

[MUSIC NO. 02 "VINETTE'S ENTRANCE"]

She was lightning over a picnic...

She was waterfall in the clearing...

She was river stream in a mountain...

She was just an absolute babe!

Took myself by the scruff of the neck and said why not take a chance and lyric this siren? Scored this organic carrot juice and plopped it down in front a her, just the right amount of charm and juss the right amount of baritone to my arm.

She pretend she ain't surprised but then she tip them shades low on to her nose and

She look at me like,

VINETTE. How you know I like carrot juice?

KLOOK. And I tell her because I know your every need before you do.

VINETTE. Oh you do?

KLOOK. Juss got it like that.

VINETTE. Oh you do?

KLOOK. Told the fella put some ginger in it but then took a longer look at your pulchritudinous self and said nah, ginger scratch up her throat.

VINETTE. Hm.

KLOOK. Right or wrong, ginger scratch up your throat?

VINETTE. Ginger does make my throat itch a little.

KLOOK. Ha!

VINETTE. But you feeling frisky and like you got my number and that makes a lady feel like giving you a hard time.

KLOOK. I can understand that.

VINETTE. A lucky carrot juice intuition does not incline me to endow you with mystical proclivities.

KLOOK. OK.

VINETTE. Feel like I should decline your carrot juice...

KLOOK. I hope you reconsider as I put my truck into reverse.

VINETTE. This what you do, accost women while bearing vegetable fluids?

KLOOK. Only the impossibly charismatic and intriguing ones.

VINETTE. Hm.

KLOOK. How'm I doing?

VINETTE. Still appraising.

KLOOK. If I'm coming on too strong then chalk it up to a lonely man grasping for hope.

VINETTE. Telling me you lonely ain't the best commercial for your product.

KLOOK. Ain't selling nothing 'cause shit this good sells itself.

VINETTE. Hm.

KLOOK. May I sit?

VINETTE. You may sit.

KLOOK. Why thank you.

VINETTE. Don't mention it.

KLOOK. Like that juice?

VINETTE. The juice is fine.

KLOOK. Good.

VINETTE. Good.

KLOOK. Mine's good also.

VINETTE. Why your eyes so sad?

KLOOK. My eyes are sad?

VINETTE. Just about the saddest eyes I ever seen.

KLOOK. In truth?

VINETTE. In truth.

KLOOK. Whyncha stay a while and less you and me talk...

VINETTE. I had blown into town on the run from myself so I could find myself.

Investigate and explore whass going in me and, and well putting it kinda bluntly stop getting involved with people and places that are not conducive to spiritual upliftment...

Wild-ass men, heh. My kryptonite.

My scar. Been some scars inflicted, by myself and others...

Don't get me wrong, I'm not no... I mean I wasn't *easy* or nothing, but...

Takes a while for us to see that who's holding us back is the person looking back at us in the mirror.

Thought I could do all that if I juss kept on the road a piece.

Was hoping to catch a job in this town I dunno like barmaid-ing, waitressing, telephone sales-ing, shop assisting, cigar rolling any damn thing juss to keep body and soul together and afford me a little headspace in order to ruminate on my next move.

I was a li'l lost, y'know? Like I might do this or I might do that... And now organic carrot juice and a man with sadness and kindness sitting on his shoulders.

This fella shone a light on me and lit me up straight away and yes, he was too old.

KLOOK. Hey!

VINETTE. And yes, he was most egregiously a man who was dragging disorder around by the tail and yes, he was most transparently gonna be a romantic catastrophe. I knew all that from when he blabbering bullshit 'bout ginger and carrots...

But what could I do? When it clicks, it clicks. So many men just looking at me but ain't seeing what I had in me.

KLOOK. I could see what she had in her!

Man
Like sunshine
And she made me charming, y'know?
Thass the thing about charm
Everyone is charming if they take enough interest in who they trying to charm
And this was an interesting deep thinking individual
Yes, she was ten years –

VINETTE. Ha.

KLOOK. OK twenty years – too young for me but who wouldn't if he could? Conversation for hours that ranged across the plains.

VINETTE. We did like to talk thass true.

KLOOK. Cuba,

VINETTE. Venezuela,

KLOOK. Michelle Alexander and *The New Jim Crow*,

VINETTE. The history of basketball and the parallels with the development of be-bop,

KLOOK. Werner Herzog,

VINETTE. Charles Burnett,

KLOOK. Joan Miró,

VINETTE. The forgotten career of Dupree Bolton,

KLOOK. Whass wrong with my man Yaphet Kotto's tongue,

VINETTE. How political language is getting so damn lazy,

KLOOK. How to cook the perfect stew chicken,

VINETTE. Why I believe vegetarianism is not only moral but could actually save the whole economy of this country,

KLOOK. Why Thomas Piketty still got it right.

VINETTE. Why I've never been that fond of movies that use flashbacks and voice-overs,

KLOOK. Why James Gandolfini is a better actor than Marlon Brando,

VINETTE. How to mix paint so it pulls across a skirting board just right,

KLOOK. Aesthetic v. anaesthetic – how one make your brain alive to the max and the other 'bout shutting down.

VINETTE. Audre Lorde,

KLOOK. Langston Hughes,

VINETTE. Andrew Marvell,

KLOOK. Leonard Gardner,

VINETTE. Vladimir Nabokov,

KLOOK. We talked about all kindsa shit.

VINETTE. Yes, we did and it flowed like a waterfall.

KLOOK. One carrot juice after another.

VINETTE. Hours flew by.

KLOOK. They flew.

VINETTE. And I can't remember every joke
But a question in his eyes
And a melancholy in his timbre thass got me fluttery right around my throat like I wanna kiss him, it was that potent.

KLOOK. I'm pretty confident that we're riding on a vibe. But I'm old enough to know that vibe ain't nothing if the timing ain't right.

VINETTE. I'm saying to myself play it cool, Vinette, don't just rush when the hand should be long
And he don't know that I don't know anyone here
So when he say –

KLOOK. I'd like to see you again

VINETTE. I twist my lips to the side like I'm thinking 'bout it and looking at him like one would inspect a secondhand motorcar, checking for the defects and he twinkling like he's saying you'd be crazy not to take him for a spin.

KLOOK. Feel like sum'un momentous dangling on a precipice, like it might happen it might not, y'know?

[MUSIC NO. 03 "TIME CRYSTAL TIME"]

KLOOK.
    TIME
    CRYSTAL
    TIME

DON'T MOVE IT ON
STOP TIME,
THIS MOMENT NOW
STOP TIME

VINETTE.
BEFORE THE BLUSH
THERE IS A SIGH OH
BEFORE THE RAIN,
THERE IS A CRY
A SEED IS CARRIED ON THE WIND
AND JUST BEFORE A KISS,
THE HURRICANE OF LOVE BEGINS

KLOOK.
TIME
CRYSTAL
TIME
DON'T MOVE IT ON
STOP TIME,
THIS MOMENT NOW
STOP TIME

VINETTE.
THE ONES THAT CAME BEFORE,
DISAPPEARING IN THIS DAWN
A WAVE INSIDE MY CHEST
I SWAY TO LOVE'S BEHEST,
I FEEL TO TAKE A RISK,
THE DANGER AND THE BLISS,
HIS SMILE IS LIKE THE SUN,
I'M THE BULLET, HE'S THE GUN OH

KLOOK.
AND THE SCARS I HOLD,
THE SHACKLES ON MY SOUL
MELT FROM MY HEART
A NEW MOVEMENT, A NEW START
FEAR DON'T SLOW ME DOWN
BECAUSE THE MOMENT IT IS NOW
A LIFETIME OF REGRET
BUT IT HASN'T KILLED ME YET, YEAH

KLOOK. I'm asking for her number and I ain't even got a phone my damn self, just older than old school holding out a napkin and telling her write it on that.

VINETTE. This sad-eyed fella don't even got a pen.

KLOOK. I ask the waitress.

VINETTE. But I have an eyeliner pencil at the bottom of my bag.

KLOOK. She's leaning over to write it and I swear to God I ain't felt like this since my teenage years in south Atlanta.

VINETTE. A moment of hesitation.

KLOOK. I sense her pulling back.

VINETTE. But then I write it.

KLOOK. Yup, yup!

VINETTE. And the moment is done I feel right.

KLOOK.
>TIME
>CRYSTAL
>TIME
>DON'T MOVE IT ON
>STOP TIME,
>THIS MOMENT NOW
>STOP TIME

VINETTE.
>BEFORE THE BLUSH
>THERE IS A SIGH OH
>BEFORE THE RAIN,
>THERE IS A CRY
>A SEED IS CARRIED IN THE AIR
>AND JUST BEFORE A KISS,
>THE HURRICANE GOT ME SCARED

KLOOK. Had a steady job at the time cleaning swimming pools in a health club where people using that club were most certainly not the most healthy looking people kinda people, didn't seem to have no idea of work or pressure or if they did they sure knew how to hide it 'cause they were there every day juss barbecuing their torsos and drinking.

I've had worse gigs, y'know? Man gotta work... And Vinette, she –

VINETTE. I'm staying on his couch and not letting nothing happen between us even though iss hard to fight I'm letting him kiss me now but he still sleeping in his own room with a door firm shut and chair propped up against it in case he can't be a gentleman.

KLOOK. She couldn't leave me alone! I had to tell her to slow down, to let our love unfold like the single petal of a rose but man she was like a damn tigress! I had to lock my door at night and she scratching them captivating fingernails on the door... Man could just about go insane. And of course I wilted eventually.

VINETTE. He was so insistent and persistent that he wore down my resistance.

We took to his bed couple nights into it and I still feeling uneasy but it just felt right... What to say?

KLOOK. The key fit the lock.

VINETTE. More than that. We opened ourselves to each other and we honored what we had to give.

KLOOK. Took our damn time and did it the way iss s'posed to be done, y'know?

VINETTE. Yes, we did.

KLOOK. We took it to the realm where our bodies don't hold no weight and where we taste with our ears and hear with our tongues.

VINETTE. Taste with our ears.

KLOOK. Hear with our tongues
See with our hands
Touch with our eyes.

VINETTE. Love like psyllicybin.

[MUSIC NO. 04 "TASTE WITH OUR EARS"]

KLOOK & VINETTE.
TASTE WITH OUR EARS
HEAR WITH OUR TONGUES
SEE WITH OUR HANDS

>
> TOUCH WITH OUR EYES
> TASTE WITH OUR EARS
> HEAR WITH OUR TONGUES
> SEE WITH OUR HANDS
> TOUCH WITH OUR EYES.

VINETTE.   **KLOOK.**

VINETTE	KLOOK
TASTE WITH OUR EARS	TASTE WITH OUR EARS
	HEAR WITH OUR TONGUES
HEAR WITH OUR TONGUES	SEE WITH OUR HANDS
	TOUCH WITH OUR EYES
SEE WITH OUR HANDS	TASTE WITH OUR EARS
	HEAR WITH OUR TONGUES
TOUCH WITH OUR EYES	SEE WITH OUR HANDS
	TOUCH WITH OUR EYES

VINETTE. Felt like I took his liver and made it my face…
> Violently in love and tripping out on the oneness…
> Our oneness, y'know?
>
> We were long-lost twins or something, crawling back into a womb of our own design… A darkness to it and more than a little perfume of sorrow to our sheets… But we kept on doing it and doing it 'til we both were sobbing.

KLOOK. We are seventeen feet tall
> We are rainforests
> We are verdant and dense
> A tree grows from me to her
> We form a canopy round each other
> Our roots drink deep from the wounded soil
>
> Our hearts are raining
> We catch the rain upon our starving tongues
> Each kiss is a balm
> Each caress is a salve.

VINETTE. And when dawn tickled our eyes we knew we had become statues.

KLOOK. We had become godlike.

VINETTE. Like we was here in the lava when the earth was getting born.

KLOOK. Like we were from outer space and colonizing a new planet.

VINETTE. Man, love is good when iss right.

KLOOK. She made me into a mountain.

VINETTE. He made me into a breeze.

KLOOK. I loved her like a comet.

VINETTE. I loved him like sound.

KLOOK. Cooked her up some huevos rancheros I'd learnt to cook in Guadalajara... Oh man, Guadalajara, now thass another fable for another time frame... Avocado kinda tough but it still represent.

VINETTE. Them eggs was the most nutritious thing I ever ate in my whole entire life.

[MUSIC NO. 04A "THEM EGGS"]

KLOOK. We both naked abed and chomping on eggs.

VINETTE. And my eyes sting to look at him.

KLOOK. And my heart shaking the whole room.

VINETTE. The mind says, "Couldn't last," and the soul says, "Shut up and enjoy this."

KLOOK. And she looking at my nakedness and she asking me 'bout which scar belong to which sorrow.

VINETTE. And he looking at my nakedness and asking me 'bout when I grew which part.

KLOOK. And which of my tattoos I got in which city.

VINETTE. Exhilaration to this shit, y'know.

KLOOK. And I bless her every inch.

VINETTE. And I bless every woman who's kissed his body before me.

KLOOK. And I can see her bereavement and her fury evaporating like steam off a pie.

VINETTE. And the silence is music.

KLOOK. And the stillness is dance.

VINETTE. Could this old motherfucker be the one?

KLOOK. Could this young motherfucker be the one?

VINETTE. And then he probed too far.

KLOOK. That a stretch mark?

VINETTE. Huh?

KLOOK. Like you had a kid.

VINETTE. Hm.

KLOOK. You got a kid?

VINETTE. Yeah.

KLOOK. Where your kid?

VINETTE. Home with his gramma.

KLOOK. Boy?

VINETTE. Uh-huh.

KLOOK. Don'tcha miss him?

VINETTE. Uh-huh.

KLOOK. Well, why you ain't with him?

VINETTE. The spell snaps, and so do I.
   WHY YOU PRYING INTO ALLA THAT?

KLOOK. Pryi –?

VINETTE. Prying like a cop!

KLOOK. I ain't no –

VINETTE. Prying like a priest!

KLOOK. Vinette?

VINETTE. No "Vinette"!
   Everybody gotta stick their nose into my shit like damn dogs, sniff, sniff, sniff, get the FUCK OUT!

KLOOK. Whoa...

VINETTE. Judging me, judging me, yes thass right I had a kid! I had a kid with a useless, wild-ass dude who don't know how to tie his own shoes and once I got free a him I was left with a frog in a blanket depending on me for his life and me looking down and feeling a half-inch tall and all my dreams like mulch and now I left the kid with my mother, OK, she got him, because thass the kinda shitty kinda woman I am! OK? Done prying? Want me to scrape my skin off my face and let you eat it? Got all you need? Jesus.

KLOOK. Hey, I don't mean to pry…

VINETTE. Think it ain't a weight on my mind? Iss ALWAYS on my mind.

    (Pause.)

Guess you looking for an apology now 'cause I juss exploded at you.

KLOOK. I'm not really sure what I'm looking for.

VINETTE. I'll give you an apology then, whether you want it or not.

KLOOK. … OK…

VINETTE. Thass it. I juss gave it.

KLOOK. Well then I appreciate it.

VINETTE. Iss juss a giant confusion thass all.

KLOOK. Well, less kick its ass and never touch it again.

VINETTE. I'll tell you some…

I don't think I have it in me to be a parent.

KLOOK. I find that hard to believe, someone as warm as you are.

VINETTE. No… I look at the boy and I know I s'posed to wanna wrap him up but the fear juss suffocate and I have to…to *go*… And of course his face and voice are always with me but… I juss can't make that scene…

KLOOK. You got so much to give, Vinette…

[MUSIC NO. 05 "FRAGILE"]

    FRAGILE

VINETTE.

    FRAGILE

KLOOK. But in this day.

VINETTE.

    BUT IN THIS DAY

KLOOK & VINETTE.
>SOMETHING SINGS IN ME
>AND WE FLY,
>AND WE DANCE,
>AND THE FUTURE CAN BE HELD
>THE FUTURE CAN BE HELD OFF.

VINETTE. Taking off a mask can burn up your face if iss done too fast
But Klook…
Klook so tender
Klook like a surgeon taking off my bandages one layer at a time
And when the last layer come off

KLOOK & VINETTE.
>HE SHOW ME MYSELF

VINETTE. And myself looking so pretty on the inside.

KLOOK.
>FRAGILE

VINETTE.
>FRAGILE

KLOOK. But now tonight.

VINETTE.
>AND NOW TONIGHT,

KLOOK.
>SOMETHING LIVES IN ME

KLOOK & VINETTE.
>AND WE SWIM,
>AND WE SING,
>AND THE FUTURE CAN BE LOVE
>THE FUTURE CAN BE HELD OFF…

VINETTE. Now I know that it ain't right to seek affirmation and approbation, I know we s'posed to do that for ourselves, I know that…
But it doesn't hurt when a kindly soul like Klook offering beatitudes and benedictions…
One mask after another…

'Til the mask I don't wanna take off...

The mask hiding *me*...

KLOOK. Whass dis?

VINETTE. Hm?

KLOOK. This writing here...

VINETTE. Ah.

KLOOK. Looking like a story, sum'un like that.

VINETTE. No!

KLOOK. What?

VINETTE. Put that down straight away!

KLOOK. Whafor?

VINETTE. Iss private!

KLOOK. What is it?

VINETTE. None a your bizness!

KLOOK. Whoa... Juss cool... Here you go...

I ain't sticking my snout into no trough, take it and godspeed, girl, shit.

VINETTE. Sorry... Iss juss...

Klook...

Iss my...

Iss my writing...

(Pause.)

KLOOK. Iss your what?

VINETTE. My writing. I was, uh, I was tryna write. Used to, y'know...try and write.

KLOOK. Been tryna write what?

VINETTE. Don't laugh, alright...

KLOOK. Promise.

VINETTE. I used to have this idea in my head...

That I can write fiction...

Short stories...

KLOOK. Cool.

VINETTE. I said don't laugh.

KLOOK. Ain't laughing.

VINETTE. I put 'em aside, iss juss some bullshit dream, y'know, like being a popular music star sum'un… Dunno why I ain't throw 'em out juss yet…
They're no good.

KLOOK. Who sez they're no good?

VINETTE. Truss me, they're no good.

KLOOK. Who sez?

VINETTE. I do! I put 'em in a drawer and pulled 'em out and read 'em, y'know, like they were written by someone else and…

KLOOK. And what?

VINETTE. Flat. Dull. No life.

KLOOK. I find that extremely hard to believe.

VINETTE. Less talk about some other shit, OK? This shit… Kinda gets to me deep and I'd rather forget about it.

(Pause.)

What?

KLOOK. Ain't said nothing!

VINETTE. No, but you thinking something loud, I can see it in your face.

KLOOK. I assure you I don't have a single thought in my head.

VINETTE. You better tell me what you got running through that damn enigmatic mind of yours before I hurl one of them trucks at you.

KLOOK. I'm thinking what you're thinking but ain't ready to give voice to yet.

VINETTE. Oh really?

KLOOK. Pick 'em up and fix 'em.

VINETTE. Klook…

KLOOK. I'm serious!

VINETTE. Lissen… Writers… Always been from…

KLOOK. Bullshit.

VINETTE. I ain't even said it!

KLOOK. Bullshit. You don't need to come from.

VINETTE. And my schooling was...

KLOOK. Lemme tell yuh sum'un 'bout schools –

VINETTE. School like prison.

KLOOK. *(Overlap.)* School ain't like no –

VINETTE. School like strangulation

School like a coffin

School like death

One time they gimme a book to read and I stayed up all night to read it and I ain't never had a feeling like it in my life just made me fly out my body y'know, the words and the people and the world of the mind, but when I'm s'posed to write about it I couldn't do it, like my thoughts about it are too much of me on the page, and I told the teacher I didn't read it even though I had devoured it and he put me in the slow stream with all the messed up kids with no future and thass what I became because one thing I learned was not to show no smarts at all, that made you a target, and the slow terror and the self-hatred and then I'm out the door with a joint and a boy and never turning back and iss leff a mark on me, y'know, leff a stain and it ain't really leff me with

Leff me with

Ah, forget it.

KLOOK. Tell me.

VINETTE. Ain't really leff me with a whole lotta self-belief when it comes to a creative life, y'know?

KLOOK. Butchou wrote 'em.

VINETTE. So what? Used to grab a hairbrush and sing in a mirror too.

KLOOK. Butchou ain't throw 'em out when you coulda so whatchou hanging on to them for?

VINETTE. I 'on't know...

KLOOK. Vinette... Look how you talk. Spellbinds my heart and you paint the pictures in my mind every time. Pick up a pen, or flip open your damn Macbook, and get these stories outchour head and into the world…

VINETTE. So simple, huh?

KLOOK. Yeah, simple.

But the hardest thing in this world is to keep our shit simple.

But keep it simple.

VINETTE. Hm.

KLOOK. You must not give up.

VINETTE. Go to work.

KLOOK. Don't give up.

VINETTE. Getchourself to work.

KLOOK. Man I worked for was the most finickety fuck I ever worked for in my life… Juss took a dislike to me from the get-go… Said I stank a marijuana when I ain't had a joint since I was managing a lounge bar in Cleveland! And thass a long time ago.

Up my ass all day and all night 'bout the leaves in the pool and towels in the hut…

Howard was his name…

Lemme tell you something.

Don't never trust a man who shapes his beard.

Dude had his beard like this, all thin 'round his chin then coming up round his lips like he drew it on. One time I said to him, "How long it take you to shave that thing in the morning?" And he lit up like a motherfuckin' Christmas tree like I was admiring it and I realize to my dismay that I hit on his favorite subject – his beard. He tell me 'bout he try it this way and how he had to get these special clippers with the extra fine edge and he used to shape it like this – shows me picture – and then he shape it like this – shows me picture – and now he's trying it like it is now and I'm nodding my head thinking, please kill me. The guy just rubbed me all kindsa wrong ways, y'know? Like he brought me out in a rash and shit. And then one time Vinette springs up at work –

VINETTE. I was on my way to the library to return some Roxane Gay and thought I'd say hello.

KLOOK. Howard stop still and stares like a laser beam.

VINETTE. Yeah, he was weird…

KLOOK. Looking at her like she's a honey glazed ham…

VINETTE. I'm tryna stay polite but the truth is Howard had something wrong with him when it came to women.

KLOOK. Howard like he lost the power of speech.

VINETTE. I just say hey to Klook and then I'm outta there. I can feel Howard's eyes burning into my ass as I walk away.

KLOOK. See, here's the thing… If he had said one thing, made one comment… But he didn't… It was just a look, a vibe, a…

VINETTE. Creepy, creepy, creepy, creepy…

KLOOK. So I couldn't call the motherfucker to account but…I'm making a mental note… Howard has dark and dangerous desires that could might…flare up…and would have to be addressed at some time…

VINETTE. Klook pulling double shifts, night shifts, and here's me just mooching around at home…

Staring at the trucks raising up dust rattling my windows…

And something

SOMETHING SINGS IN ME…

Them stories…

Them stories nagging at me like a baby crying through a thin wall…

Got them teachers in my head with their pernicious imprint on me.

Shame is what they left in me, shame and fear – all up in my bloodstream, y'know…

Shame and fear and a feeling like don't get above y'self so you don't get crushed…

Shame and fear…

Got family voices in my head

Telling me why bother, even trying to think and breathe, you can't you can't but…

Klook in my head, his voice in my head saying,

KLOOK. You can, you can.

[MUSIC NO. 06 "I PICK 'EM UP"]

VINETTE. I pick 'em up.

Refine 'em.

Cut 'em down…

And…

They…

They get better.

Slowly, inexorably…

Not so clunky, y'know?

But when it comes time to sharing the page…

I couldn't

I just couldn't let him read it…

Like showing him the most hidden, most private, pinkest wound…

Man, this ain't easy!

KLOOK. Howard the Beard juss wouldn't let up on me, y'know?

"Done this? Seen to that?"

Relentless. Right up my ass the livelong day.

He got mad 'cause I walk in on him one time and he's… Ah, how to put this delicately… Peeping at the chicks by the pool and, ah, pleasuring himself…

He all jumping in the air and straightening out the papers on his desk but thass what he was doing…

Made him even tougher on me.

Howard one a them little men like to try to make a big man look small. Ah!

Bite my tongue and clench my teeth and more than once come home in a murky mood, and much as I try to protect her from my vexations, man, I ain't no saint when it come to patience and the walls in that place was mad close.

VINETTE. So there was a strain. Absolutely there was a strain. But then I'd be staring out the window at the trucks and the hitchers and he'd suddenly sneak up on me kiss up my neck and there's me not even feeling his approach. Pull me into the bed and tell me he love me. Strong man never took a step off me, never backed down, juss feet planted square shoulders and take me on. Why you so good to me?

KLOOK. Why wouldn't I be good to you?

VINETTE. Because I'm no good.

KLOOK. Foolish thought to utter such nonsense.

VINETTE. I'm gonna make you feel good... You want me to make you feel good?

KLOOK. Yeah, I want you to make me feel good.

VINETTE. Hm.

KLOOK. And once you've made me feel good, I'm gonna make you feel good in return...

VINETTE. Now that... Sounds like a very good blueprint...

KLOOK. Oh, a blueprint?

VINETTE. Yeah, a blueprint...

KLOOK. Well, you can print me in blue.

VINETTE. And I reach into my drawer, the one he clear out for me... I got something silk in there because I'm in the mood to plant my flag on my man... Make him remember how good a human being can feel...
But as my hand fumble for the silk...
I feel something metal.
Something not like life.
Something metal and the opposite of life.

KLOOK. She found my fire stick.
My Colt 45, instrument of death.

VINETTE. I bring it out and there's a ski mask, raggedy old thing like him, wrapped around the 45 like a comfort blanket. My mouth dry but my tongue cracks enough to say, what the hell you doing with this?

KLOOK. I tell her thass juss a distant tremor from a long dead past.

VINETTE. I say past my ass! This don't feel like no distant tremor, this feels like some cold hard factual present, some nowness, right here in the drawer where I keep my silk. What the hell you doing with this?

KLOOK. And the first twenty-five years of my life cascading off my tongue and into the room.

Orphanage.

Victimized and brutalized.

Bare knuckles leads to brass knuckles.

Baseball bat leads to iron bar leads to shank leads to shiv leads to a 32 snubnose in the waistband.

Reform school.

Gang leader.

Mugging leads to stick-ups leads to armed robbery leads to prison.

Fighting in the yard leads to carnage on the staircase leads to solitary leads to insanity.

And now a life is adopted and a soul is corrupted,

A burglary,

A bank job,

A credit card scam,

Holding up a truck,

Selling stolen cigarettes then prison,

Release,

Short order cook but fired, janitor but fired,

Carpenter but fired,

Taxi driver but fired,

Then

Bad things abounding in the alleyways

Finger breaking

Arm breaking,
Leg breakin' and some head breaking
Washing blood off my knuckles on the daily
An extortion ring,
A cocaine ring,
A ganja ring,
Every city and every state and some overseas to boot, and thank God I ain't get **catch** after Slick Willy Clinton bring in his three strikes and you're out fascist bullshit. When I lay it out end to end like that, like the sum of my life…
I gotta admit it sounds real, real worryingly bad…

VINETTE. I say, man!
This is like…finding a deadly cobra in your dressing gown pocket.

KLOOK. My head is on the block and guillotine done primed.

VINETTE. I juss can't carry that kinda calamity, Klook.

KLOOK. You ain't gonna carry no calamity.

VINETTE. I'm sitting here feeling like I finally found a sanctuary and this…violence…so close to where I live…

KLOOK. I know it sounds bad just boiled down…but there's a political dimension to a life such as mine.

VINETTE. Political dimens –!
Politics ain't make you hit no little old lady on her head.

KLOOK. I ain't never hit no li'l ol' –

VINETTE. Politics ain't make you carrying on like a damn crazy man, lotsa people coming up just as hard and they ain't running round with ski mask and death stick Politics ain't done none a that, you done alla that.

KLOOK. Vinette… My Vinette… That was who I was, not who I am.

VINETTE. No, Klook… Who we was is always who we are…

KLOOK. And since we been spending time together, you seen me lose my cool with anyone? See me get hot 'bout anything? You the one getting hot, damn near bit my head clean off when I asked you 'bout that boy you got back at your mother's –

VINETTE. *(Overlap from "See me get hot.")* If you in love with death and all that means, then you can't be in love wimme and that means, hard as it is to say it, that I cannot –

CAN NOT be in love widjou.

Here's me tryna change my circumstance and not repeat some injurious self-inflicted bullshit and now here you are and I can't tell if you got horns or a halo top your head.

KLOOK. *(Overlap from "Circumstance.")* How can you be satisfied? I don't think you can. You just gotta go on what your deepest insides are telling you to do.

When I did all that wrongness, thass when I couldn't speak, hadn't learned to speak...

And now I learned to speak

And iss you that showed me how to speak.

Don't turn away from the peace we found

I know you see whass inside me like x-ray vision, like we been reincarnated from another time.

VINETTE. *(Overlap from "Thass when I couldn't speak.")* Talk and talk but you ain't saying nothing but talk, you want me to put my injuries in your hands, but your hands been aiming death on peaceful people like myself and ain't no way you gonna change, this is 'xackly why I got on the highway in the first place so I wouldn't get myself embroiled and now here I am staring embroiled right in the face, nah man, no can do, sorry but I gots to go...

KLOOK. *(Overlap from "Highway in the first place.")* At my age, I'm gonna do another bid?

With my knees and my disposition?

Vinette.

VINETTE. I can't.

KLOOK. Vinette.

VINETTE. I can't.

[MUSIC NO. 07 "AM I IN YOUR HEART?"]

KLOOK.
> AM I IN YOUR HEART?
> CAN I BE FORGIVEN?
> AM I IN YOUR HEART?
> I KNOW I LET YOU DOWN
> GIRL, I WOULD NEVER HURT YOU
> OR DESERT YOU
> YOU KNOW YOU ARE THE BEST IN ME
> AM I IN YOUR HEART? AH

I've paid. Haven't I? Knowin' what I used to be, thass worse than prison food. Thass in me, I'm carrying it.
Head fulla cobras and a heart fulla grief.
But.
Gotta be a point where I can juss be me. No?

VINETTE. Why you ain't told me before?

KLOOK. Because it was beautiful to juss have somcone take me as they find me juss once and not have to... Thass all. I'm not... Please...

VINETTE. Why you still got the gun and the mask if iss all in the past?

KLOOK. I –

VINETTE. Yes?

KLOOK. I juss forgot to throw it out.

VINETTE. Thass weak, Klook.

KLOOK. Iss all I got.

VINETTE. It ain't a lot.

KLOOK.
> AM I IN YOUR HEART?
> CAN I BE FORGIVEN?
> AM I IN YOUR HEART?
> I KNOW I LET YOU DOWN
> GIRL, I WOULD NEVER HURT YOU
> OR DESERT YOU

>   YOU KNOW YOU ARE THE BEST IN ME
>   YOU ARE IN MY HEART AH

VINETTE. This whole thing feels like corrosion and moral narcolepsy right here in my face… This is antithetical to how I wanna live, Klook…

KLOOK. You have to gimme a chance… The benefit…

VINETTE. Oh Klook… You dropping some worrisome shit on my head…

KLOOK. I would never go back.

VINETTE. Hm.

KLOOK. Still appraising?

VINETTE. Still appraising.

KLOOK. C'mon back to your old motherfucker.

VINETTE. This stuff is over?

KLOOK. It's over like a sweaty dream.

VINETTE. I mean, over?

KLOOK. It's over like stonewashed jeans.
And I know you been working on them stories.

VINETTE. No, I haven't!

KLOOK. Watched you… Seen the way your mouth moves while you writing… Iss writing, no?

VINETTE. Maybe.

KLOOK. Writing stories.

VINETTE. …Yyyeeahh…

KLOOK. So yuh picked 'em up like I said you should.

VINETTE. Why we talking 'bout this now when I'm so angry at you I could shit?

KLOOK. Feel good about 'em?

VINETTE. Shut up.

KLOOK. Whyncha read me one a them stories?

VINETTE. Stop wid da stories…

KLOOK. Serious. Read one to me. I would be so very deeply honored to know whass on your mind.

VINETTE. If thass juss mouth music you speaking…

KLOOK. It ain't mouth music.

VINETTE. I 'on't know…

This some personal shit right here on this page, Klook…

KLOOK. S'up to you, mistress.

VINETTE. *(To audience.)* I'm still scared and apprehensive and more than a little miffed about the fire stick, but…

KLOOK. She's coming back, I can feel the cord again.

VINETTE. But I ain't reading them out loud, you old motherfucker, you turn that damn radio off, getchour mind straight and sit there with a beer and read it to y'self…

And he gets hisself comfortable and turns the page and I am utterly defenseless and exposed…

He shake his head softly like he got a fly on his cheek or like he can't believe what he just read…

Can't believe how good it is or how terrible?

[MUSIC NO. 08 "NOW YOU SEE"]

NOW YOU SEE THE TRUTH IN ME
THE LOSS IN MY HEART AND THE INVISIBLE SCARS.
NOW YOU SEE THE TRUTH IN ME AND I FEAR WHAT
   YOU'LL SAY
PLEASE DON'T TURN AWAY

ME AND MY HISTORY DONE SEEN THINGS
I WISH I COULD UNSEE
ME AND MY HISTORY, DONE BEEN THINGS
I WISH I COULD UN-BE, UN-BE

OH
NOW YOU SEE THE TRUTH IN ME
AND I FEAR WHAT YOU'LL SAY
'CAUSE I NEED YOU TO STAY

NOW YOU SEE THE TRUTH IN ME,
WATCH YOU READ THROUGH MY WORDS,
NO DEFENSE, YOU'RE THE FIRST

ME AND MY HISTORY DONE SEEN THINGS
I WISH I COULD UNSEE

ME AND MY HISTORY, I HAVE BEEN THINGS
I WISH I COULD UN-BE

NOW YOU SEE
NOW YOU SEE
NOW YOU SEE

KLOOK. Water and salt from my eyes bless the page and make it splotched...

I turn to my love...

VINETTE. Whadjuh make of it, honey?

KLOOK. Girl...

This is...

This is...

VINETTE. Yeah?

KLOOK. I ain't no expert on nonea this stuff... I mean I read some Chester Himes, Albert Camus, little Dostoevsky, some Bertrand Russell once on a bid I pulled in San Quentin or Riker's Island, I forget which...

But

This

This is

THIS IS SOME GOOD SHIT

I mean, you really mean what you saying and you don't miss a thing, like when you say the old man hair trying to scape off his head like a cumulus.

That shit is good.

VINETTE. You think so?

You the first one to look at it

AND WHAT YOU THINK MEANS MORE TO ME THAN THE SUN COMING UP

KLOOK. I'm sitting in here with some sorta literary genius.

You're a giant, girl.

All this time I'm juss going 'bout my business with you and you got a giant living in your mind.

And I talk through them stories she wrote,

VINETTE. And I talk 'bout where they come from the talk keep talking and the memories shimmering and the ideas twisting.

KLOOK. And this is like making love but we ain't even touching iss juss stories.

VINETTE. I tell him 'bout the father of my son, how he was a young teacher, fresh from college and idealistic and shit gonna change society and how much he showed to me and how sad it was that he had so much rage that he couldn't contain and how I told him I couldn't understand how he could inspire a room full a kids and then come back and put me down for hours upon hours and me having to question within, like, why am I taking it lying down and what that say 'bout me?

And how hard it was to push on up 'specially with the young teacher growing inside me but it had to be done because it was heading worse and worse.

I never spoke that way so free to one person ever in my life.

KLOOK. And I tell her some funny things also, like when I did four years in Parchman and there was this fly just buzzing and buzzing in my cell fit to drive a man insane and how I'm flicking at this damn fly with a t-shirt and wrecking my cell and finally I get all zen and kung fu 'bout it and breathe and close my eyes and then *zzttt* catch it in my hand but steada juss killing it I let it go because a something I realize, all these men liffin' weights to be a deterrent but me I'm working on speed, so me and this fly start training together the fly buzzing and me breathing and tryna figure him out before he figures me out and then *zzztt*.

Catch him in my hand. Got so I was so fast wid ma hands that no one fucked wimme in there. They knew not to 'cause I'd break they damn nose before they blink. And I ain't that big a guy, look. And when that fly finally passed away, I held a funeral for my friend and buried him at sea...well...flushed his little ass down the toilet.

VINETTE. The more we talked and the later it got, the stronger I felt, and the more awake I became. A night of magic.

KLOOK. 'Til dawn sticking her rosy red fingers round that Venetian and the trucks commence to roaring and rattling our room and I gotta hit work with no sleep.

VINETTE. Before you go, though...wanna meet my boy?

KLOOK. He's here?

VINETTE. On Skype, stoopid!

KLOOK. Ah!

VINETTE. You'll love him.

KLOOK. Of course I will, he came outta you.

VINETTE. Little pitbull of a dude.

KLOOK. You gave birth to a pitbull?

VINETTE. You ready?

KLOOK. Yes, I am ready.

VINETTE. He comes online, pixels and messed up sound can't dilute his beauty.

KLOOK. He's a great kid. Funny and sparky and got questions galore.

VINETTE. It breaks my heart and makes it strong all at the same time and best of all is how he talks to Klook.

KLOOK. Little boy sticking his tongue out at me and I'm sticking my tongue at him and we both laughing and iss juss no effort because li'l fella got enchantment radiating from him and of course I can't help but think 'bout my own little self long ago in the past and it strikes me that this li'l fella gotta have a better shot. Send for the boy.

[MUSIC NO. 09 "SEND FOR THE BOY"]

VINETTE. I will.

KLOOK. Start looking for a bigger spot so the kid got room to play with his toys.

VINETTE. Klook...

KLOOK. It's good, this thing.

VINETTE. Klook, I –

KLOOK. It's good.

And even Howard's stupid beard and the red blobs by the pool can't blow my high after that night.

Sex of the mind

Those words!

Spend the day in a reverie

And images and phrases and the lyrics of our talk come back to me like drowsy bees.

Walk into Howard's office, he looking at some nasty website, "Barely Legal Teens Debased For Your Delight," room got that cheesy jizzy aroma I know so well from prison and he asking me if I repaired the pool filter and changed the bulb in the bar fridge and I say yes and then he asks me a whole bunch of other shit like he gonna catch me out but I done it all.

Then he asks me how my girl is…

A silence…

Every muscle in me wanting to karate chop his throat collapse his Adam's apple then stomp on his ribcage because we both know what he's saying when he asks that, he's saying he wants to fuck her,

But I just say

She's cool

Howard leans back on his chair eyes flicking back to some terrified teen on his laptop and I leave.

And some blob talking 'bout could I get her an ice cold Corona and some factor forty-five Coppertone and I say sorry mam I'm the maintenance man that means I do the maintenance y'know

Maintaining

But if you look out for Carlos he'll set you up, and she takes off her sunglass and shoot me a look thass s'posed to be haughty and

Then she sez,

"I told you what I want, now get me what I want."

I'm 'bout to drop seven or eight justly chosen cuss words on her incarnadine ass, but I tell her you know what, iss a lovely day and I'm having a rare time of feeling hopeful and happy, so why don't we juss agree to be good friends and if I run up on Carlos I'll tell him what you want and he can take care of any needs but this fat blob got meanness in her that I seen twenty thousand times before... No sense tryna talk to them so juss tiptoe away take a deep breath and 'member what I got to hold on to when the moon rise tonight...

VINETTE. Klook heads off for work and I take that nasty hunk of death giving metal and I'm 'bout to throw it out but there's a...

Jackal or hyena or wolf, I dunno, some creature like that drilling his yellow eyes into me and tongue flopping around juss by the trash cans and it makes me shiver so I back up into our room and jam the fire stick behind the cistern in the bathroom, Pacino-style. Deal with it later when the creature has gone...

And I gotta hit the printers but the wolf, jackal hyena whatever the fuck is still there so I pitch an old coffee can at him catch him square on his head and he slink off and I get to the bus stop...

No e-mail, old school

The Collected Stories of Vinette Vasquez

Gonna mail the manuscript to some names I researched

Cold calling

They gonna know my name soon enough

The manuscript slides through the mailbox and a baby deer bucking in my chest

Carrot juice right in the spot we met and I read some Countee Cullen and pick up some limes and peppers because tonight on that tiny kitchen counter next to the rusty hot plate, I'm gonna prepare him some a my world-famous legendary vegetarian ceviche – he cooks every night but tonight I'm gonna show him what he means to me and my mind's eye already headed towards the drawer where I planted my silk.

[MUSIC NO. 10 "NEOPHYTE LOVE"]

NEOPHYTE LOVE
METEORITE LOVE
IT'S GETTING KIND OF LATE,
BEEN WAITING FOR MY MAN ALL DAY
BEEN COOKIN' UP A STORM
AND TRYNA KEEP THIS WARMTH AT BAY
MY LIPS BEGIN TO BURN
MY BODY STARTS TO YEARN
I'M HOPING THAT HE'S ON HIS WAY TO
MESMERIZE ME
TENDERIZE ME
WHAT WON'T I DO WHEN HE COMES HOME,
I'M GONNA LOVE THAT MAN
WHAT WON'T I DO WHEN HE COMES OVER AND OVER
   AND OH –
WHAT WON'T I DO WHEN HE COMES I'M GONNA LOVE
   THAT MAN
NEOPHYTE LOVE
METEORITE LOVE
I'VE GIVEN UP MY HEART,
MY HEAD AIN'T FAR BEHIND,
GOT ME THINKING THOUGHTS YOU KNOW,
MY BODY WANTS TO FEEL
HIS FINGERS IN MY HAIR,
WHEN YOU GIVE YOU GET TO SHARE,
TO SHARE,
TO SHARE
OH, WHAT WON'T I DO WHEN HE COMES HOME,
I'M GONNA LOVE THAT MAN
WHAT WON'T I DO WHEN HE COMES
OVER AND OVER AND OH,
WHAT WON'T I DO WHEN HE COMES HOME,
I'M GONNA LOVE THAT MAN
MESMERIZE ME
TENDERIZE
WHAT WON'T I DO
WHAT WON'T I DO

WHAT WON'T I DO
WHAT WON'T I DO
WHAT WON'T I DO WHEN HE COMES HOME

(**KLOOK** *re-enters, mad as hell.*)

KLOOK. Fuck, fuck, fuck.

VINETTE. Klook?

KLOOK. Don't talk to me.

VINETTE. Hey now… Lemme know and I can…

KLOOK. You can't.

VINETTE. Whass troubling you?

KLOOK. Leave me be and let me breathe.

VINETTE. Why you shutting me away?

KLOOK. Because thass whass best…

VINETTE. Why?

KLOOK. Think iss prob'bly best you mosey on down the line and catch a ride somewhere else.

VINETTE. Why you being cruel?

KLOOK. I swear to God… You don't know whass inside me and if you keep with your yammering, I'm gonna show you…

VINETTE. Show me what?

KLOOK. That I'm a piece of trash juss like they say.

VINETTE. They who? Who said you were a piece of trash?

KLOOK. I say I'm a piece of trash!

VINETTE. I don't understand…

KLOOK. That prick up at the health club done let me go…

VINETTE. Whaaaat??

KLOOK. "Sassing a customer," he say…
"Sassing a customer"!
He's lucky I didn't choke the bitch.

VINETTE. Don't talk like that…

KLOOK. Fuckin' Howard, well I juss
couldn't take it any more, Vinette,
and I –

VINETTE. Oh, fuck…

KLOOK. I had to!

VINETTE. Had to what? What did you do?

KLOOK. Gripped him up by his neck and pinned him to the wall and told him

I'd shove my gun up his –

VINETTE. Please tell me you didn't.

KLOOK. Matter of fact, where's that fire stick? Need it.

VINETTE. You absolutely do not need it, beautiful!

KLOOK. Fuck it! Gimme the fire stick. Iss who I am.

VINETTE. Thass not who you are! You ain't leaving this room with no gun. Not when I only juss begun to give you whass inside me. You read them stories, them stories I never showed to nobody. You my witness in this life. Your eyes. Only ones that can fall upon me. And I am not gonna sanction you lighting up some narrow life little Mussolini who wouldn't know a graceful moment if it stuck its finger up his ass.

[MUSIC NO. 11 "YOU SHOULD LEAVE ME"]

KLOOK. You should leave me.

VINETTE.
NO, NO, NO, NO

KLOOK. You should run as far as you can

VINETTE.
WHY WOULD I DO THAT?

KLOOK. Because what you are beholding
Before you is the most disastrously dysfunctional
Ass-backwards human
Being since the dawn of time.

VINETTE.
YOU'RE MINE YOU'RE MINE, YOU

KLOOK. Poison leakin outta me…
Anytime I ever let somebody get close it go to shit.
I don't think I could stand myself if I drove you away.

VINETTE.
>SEE ME SHAKING? ROCK SOLID LOVE
>YOU'RE MINE, YOU

KLOOK. Even though I'm old?

VINETTE. Yes.

KLOOK. Even though I'm a fuck up?

VINETTE. Yuh not a fuck up but yes.

KLOOK. Even though I'm impoverished?

VINETTE. You the richest man I ever met in my life.

KLOOK. Whatchou done widdat fire stick?

VINETTE. Ain't gonna tell you but we don't need that.

KLOOK. How you know what I need and don't need?

VINETTE. I know what you need before you need it. Why not?
>THASS WHAT LOVE IS

KLOOK. Oh thass what love is.

VINETTE.
>YES, THASS WHAT MY LOVE IS

KLOOK. No shit.

VINETTE. Thass right.

KLOOK. Come here and press yourself up on me.

VINETTE.
>WHAT FOR?

KLOOK. Because I wanna feel you close.

VINETTE. You c'mhere.

KLOOK. And that ceviche was great and the night was great and she was great. Next morning I went back and I cleaned out my locker and had to hand in my uniform all that crap. Saw fifty dollars lying orphaned out by the pool house and for the first time in my life I said you know what I'm not on that purloining style, let 'em have it, I don't even need it. Regretted it later like a motherfucker when we had to live on gungo peas and rye bread for a week, but it felt good at the time. Looking in the papers and trudging door to door for any kinda work will take it out of a man, 'specially when he's lived a few years. But she was...endlessly compassionate and unstintingly supportive. Never lost her patience when I'm crying on her belly and saying I can't, I can't she juss...

VINETTE. *(Overlap.)* Shh...

KLOOK. *(Overlap.)* Shh me and tell me...

VINETTE. You can, you can...

KLOOK. I waited my whole life to meet someone like her and I still can't believe God saw fit to put her in my path.

VINETTE. Dear Vinette Vasquez, thank you for sending us your work.

Unfortunately...

KLOOK. Unfortunately what...?

VINETTE. 'Parrently my prose is jejune...

KLOOK. Jejune? Jejune? Who wrote this?

VINETTE. I 'on't know.

KLOOK. Lemme see that...

VINETTE. Doesn't matter, Klook...

KLOOK. Nah man lemme see that, this man can't juss sit at his fancy desk and pronounce from on high 'bout the merits or demerits of your work, thass...

VINETTE. Leave it, Klook... Iss alright... Stupid dream anyway... Juss a stupid dream...

KLOOK. Well, I'm sittin' down and I'm writing this fella a letter... He gonna hear what I think about him and his arrogance...

VINETTE. Leave the man. He didn't like it. Don't matter. Now where's that job section in the paper? Pass it over.

KLOOK. But... But thass your dream...

VINETTE. Not every dream has to come true, Klook.

KLOOK. But what you dream is who you are...

VINETTE. No. What job I have is who I am...

Look, the whole food store got a position, lemme hustle up and get in something professional looking and get myself down there...

KLOOK. OK, a little job juss to keep body and mind but I ain't allowing you to stop writing, no way...

VINETTE. Lemme juss get through this with some dignity, alright? I'll be OK. I wanna get down to the whole food store, might even get a discount on produce, which will help our situation.

KLOOK. Jejune...

VINETTE. Shut up, I got jobs to hunt.

KLOOK. But it was me that got lucky with a job that day. Old fella in a garage... Kind man.

Name of Reggie.

Looked me up and down and straight away knew where I'd been. I was like, man, how could you tell? And he was, like, man, how do you think I could tell? And sure, once I took him in I could see he'd also been state raised like me.

My knowledge of cars and their parts was not extensive, but he got a mind to gimme a chance. Axsed me when I could start and I said how 'bout right now and he said well let's get after it then. Much better than scooping leaves out that damn pool.

New boss say, "Cold one?" and all the angels singing couldn't sound no sweeter... It was hot, man. Sitting in his back office that doubles as his bedroom, my boss asks me 'bout Vinette...

I find it hard to talk 'bout her, like it touch me too near, but once I get to talking I can't stop...

'Bout the grace and the kindness...

And he drinks in my words and then he says... "Think you can make it last?" And thass the question been tearing at me since the beginning... I am silent... He knows my wound... And he says, "When you don't know how to sustain...

You in a world of pain..."

And I know 'xackly what he means...

Drain the dregs from the bottle a suds he gimme, and I slap his shoulder to say thank you and I'm out, realizing I'm late...

I resolve to save up some money and get the shiniest diamond ring to slip on Vinette's finger...

Stop on the way home, get some flowers... She gonna be happy when I tell her I got a job and we can make rent and not be thrown out... Open the door and what I see does not compute.

My Vinette. Shaking. Too upset to cry. Soaked in somebody blood. Gun in her hand.

VINETTE. I lick my lips and taste blood. Salty and rich. Nothing is real.

KLOOK. I try and take the gun from her hand but she holds onto it, and she don't know why she does. I close the Venetians.

I move to hold her but she pull back, sticky with blood.

I ask her what the fuck

Her mouth don't wanna work

I tell her she gotta calm down and tell me what the fuck

And finally it comes...

Something I had worried about but hadn't thought to take care of.

VINETTE. Howard.

I'm in the whole food filling out a job form and he slides up pushing a carrot juice towards me tells me he's seen me in here drinking it so he knows I like it and I don't touch it 'cause he's so weird and he says why not swing through the health club he can find some work for me and I don't say nothing just kinda nod and those eyes are looking at me revolting and I mumble and get out and wait for the bus, don't even hand in the form, pick up couple a cans a tomato from the cheap store for dinner. Coming up the drive, there's this damn wolf jackal hyena thing in the courtyard howling and barking and chasing his own tail but I slide past him and…

Open the door here.

Howard here.

Like he teleported or some shit.

He shouldn't be real, but he is. I say what you think you're doing here?

He says he has a check for your last week to give you, but then puts his arm across the doorframe and… And…

KLOOK. I think I can guess the rest.

VINETTE. I took the first couple a punches and just twisted away from them like you showed me, Klook, and all the time I'm tryna pirouette to get outta range and we get locked up together crash 'round the room end up in the bathroom and thass where I hid your…

KLOOK. Fire stick

VINETTE. And his hands ripping at me but I get my knee up and shove him back thank God I'm wearing jeans and he's coming back at me and I got one hand clamped on his face tryna gouge out his eyeball and the other scrambling for the stick. I get my hand on it put it to his heart and…

KLOOK. Lord God.

VINETTE. The way he crumpled…

KLOOK. Where you put him?

VINETTE. Dragged him into the shower

KLOOK. Sure he's dead?

VINETTE. Unless he's undead, he's dead.

KLOOK. He's all twisted up on the tiles.

Legs this way, arms that way, nothing looks right.

Eyes still open.

Looks like he seen something he couldn't make sense of.

And the dismal mathematics of our situation smack me in my face.

I've roughed him up in his office and screamed that I was gonna shoot him...

He's dropping my last check to my home like a decent employer...

I have criminal convictions going back decades...

My history rears up, incinerates every last hope.

VINETTE. Slowly it's coming to me what I done. I look at Klook.

[MUSIC NO. 12 "HIT THE HIGHWAY"]

KLOOK & VINETTE.
OH OH OH
OH OH OH

VINETTE.
TOOK A LIFE AND NOW I'LL HAVE TO PAY
LOOKED HIM IN THE EYE AND SENT HIM DOWN TO HELL

KLOOK. Vinette, you gotta listen to me.

VINETTE.
DOWN TO HELL

VINETTE.	**KLOOK.**
TOOK A LIFE NOW I'LL BE LOCKED AWAY	VINETTE
NOW IT'S ME THAT HAS TO DIE	CALM
INSIDE A CELL	DOWN
A ROTTING CELL	CALM DOWN
TELL ME WHAT TO DO	GIVE ME THE GUN, GET IN THE SHOWER
TELL ME WHAT TO DO	NEVER FORGET THIS LOVE WAS OURS

KLOOK & VINETTE.
OH OH OH
OH OH OH
OH OH OH

KLOOK.
VINETTE, I CAN FIX THIS, BABE,
JUST GIVE ME THE STICK YOU'VE GOT TO...

VINETTE. No!
KLOOK.
    YOU'VE GOT TO HIT THE HIGHWAY
VINETTE.
    I WANT TO STAY HERE
KLOOK.
    YOU'VE GOT TO HIT THE HIGHWAY

VINETTE.	**KLOOK.**
THIS CAN'T BE RIGHT	
I CAN'T STAY	YOU'VE GOT TO HIT THE HIGHWAY

KLOOK & VINETTE.
    OH OH OH
    OH OH OH
VINETTE.
    OH OH OH OH
KLOOK. Fire up my car and drive 'til you can't drive no more, then take a bus or a train 'til you set your eyes on that li'l boy of yours...
VINETTE. No... Iss me thass done it and iss me that suffers.
    OH
KLOOK. Your little boy gonna suffer too? Whass he gotta do with all this? Go, Vinette.
VINETTE.
    TELL ME WHAT TO DO
KLOOK.
    THINK OF YOUR SON, YOU MUSTN'T LOSE HIM
VINETTE.
    TELL ME WHAT TO DO
KLOOK.
    IT AIN'T A CHOICE, YOU'VE GOT TO CHOOSE HIM
    GO, GO, GO
VINETTE.
    I WANNA STAY
KLOOK.
    GO, GO, GO

VINETTE. Oh, Klook...
KLOOK. I know... GO.

(**VINETTE** *goes.*)

The ritual commences. Half a bottle a rum in one down. Nearly heave it all back up, but shake my head and roar around the room 'til I'm straight. Back a the drawer, where the fire stick was kept, thass where I got my speed – benzedrine and a couple a other pills I dunno what the fuck are...

Never thought I'd need 'em again.

Face buzz first then my limbs...

Now I have strength. Now I can see the funny side. And it is funny. How I thought my life could be anything but this... How I thought I could ever be happy. Ain't cosmic jokes the best. Laugh like coughing blood, but laugh all the same.

Defiance of Orion, all them stars up there can suck on my balls 'cause if I can't be the master of my fate at least I can choose how I exit this dirt patch we call earth.

Click open my fire stick, check it's still functioning. Yeah. Pills and rum sing a song to my mind and I can't feel nothing and the room starting to expand and contract. Expand and contract. Such colors. Now I'm ready to do some bad things. Trucks judder.

Red and blue lights spinning.

Megaphone crackling sum'un 'bout come out with your hands up. I got plentya ammo. Plenty. Just so I can hold them off for little while, create some drama, draw them onto me. I'll take some lives and they can take mine. Bloodbath still cleans you. Fuck it. Everybody dies.

[MUSIC NO. 13 "IT HURTS / WE DON'T TELL STORIES"]

WE DON'T TELL STORIES,
STORIES THEY TELL US
WE THINK THAT WE ARE GIANTS,
WHEN WE ANTS STRUGGLING IN MUD

DON'T FORGET MY FACE,
WHEN OTHERS COME TO DANCE
FROM DAMNATION INTO GRACE,
DON'T FORGET I TOOK YOUR HAND

VINETTE.
THE HARDER YOU CHASE THE FURTHER YOUR DREAMS RECEDE,
UNTIL YOU FIND PLACE TO MAKE PEACE WITH YOUR OWN DEEDS
BUT IT HURTS STILL, YES IT HURTS STILL

AND NOW THERE ARE DAYS WHEN IT DOESN'T CROSS MY MIND
ECHOES IN SPACE, I DREAM OF A BETTER TIME
YES IT HURTS STILL, IT HURTS STILL

MY BOY LOOKS AT ME QUIZZICAL,
BECAUSE HE KNOWS THERE'S SOMETHING WRONG
THIS PAIN CAN GET TOO PHYSICAL, A DISSONANT SONG

AND HE DRAWS ME A PICTURE,
AND IT'S HIM WITH SUPER POWERS,
AND I SAY, "SHOW IT TO YOUR TEACHER"
AND HE SAYS, "NO,
IT'S OURS"

AND THAT'S WHEN I BREAK INSIDE
AND DROWN MY SON'S HEAD IN TEARS
NO THERE'S NO WAY I'LL LET HIM GO

THE HARDER YOU CHASE THE FURTHER YOUR DREAMS RECEDE,
UNTIL YOU FIND PLACE TO MAKE PEACE WITH YOUR OWN DEEDS
BUT IT HURTS STILL, YES IT HURTS STILL

My little boy asking me 'bout when he can read my new book and I say iss too scary for little boys and he tell me he's a big boy and I say oh yeah, and he say well, no one else here to protect you from the monsters and I say oh yeah thass right you are a man and he say then lemme read it and I say write your own story first and then we'll see... And then a ball bounces outside and a

friend's exhortation got him pinging into the yard like a ricochet... Book selling well...
The book is under a nom de plume...
The name on the book, the author's name, that is...
Is Klook. All that time he never told me what it stood for. Juss...
Klook. And that is enough. That will have to be...
Enough.

[MUSIC NO. 14 "FINALE (MEMORIES)"]

KLOOK & VINETTE.
> MEMORIES CASCADING
> FAKING MASQUERADING
> WHAT IS REAL? WHAT IS TRUE?
> NEON SIGN FLIPS RED TO BLUE
> LONELINESS TIES ME IN CHAINS
> SHIVER NAKED IN THE RAIN
> LIVED MY LIFE IN CRUELTY
> LIKE I'M IN A GANGSTER MOVIE
> MEMORIES, MAKE A MOCKERY
> MEMORIES KEEP ON FUCKIN' ME
> MEMORIES,
> MEMORIES,
> MEMORIES,
> MEMORIES

VINETTE. How you know I like carrot juice?

(Fade.)

End of Play

www.ingramcontent.com/pod-product-compliance
Lightning Source LLC
Chambersburg PA
CBHW051412290426
44108CB00015B/2259